THIS INSPIRATIONAL COLORING BOOK BELONGS TO :

_____

_____

AF081566

© Copyright 2021 - All rights reserved.

You may not reproduce, duplicate or send the contents of this book without direct written permission from the author. You cannot hereby despite any circumstance blame the publisher or hold him or her to legal responsibility for any reparation, compensations, or monetary forfeiture owing to the information included herein, either in a direct or an indirect way.

Legal Notice: This book has copyright protection. You can use the book for personal purpose. You should not sell, use, alter, distribute, quote, take excerpts or paraphrase in part or whole the material contained in this book without obtaining the permission of the author first.

Disclaimer Notice: You must take note that the information in this document is for casual reading and entertainment purposes only.
We have made every attempt to provide accurate, up to date and reliable information. We do not express or imply guarantees of any kind. The persons who read admit that the writer is not occupied in giving legal, financial, medical or other advice. We put this book content by sourcing various places.

Please consult a licensed professional before you try any techniques shown in this book. By going through this document, the book lover comes to an agreement that under no situation is the author accountable for any forfeiture, direct or indirect, which they may incur because of the use of material contained in this document, including, but not limited to, — errors, omissions, or inaccuracies.

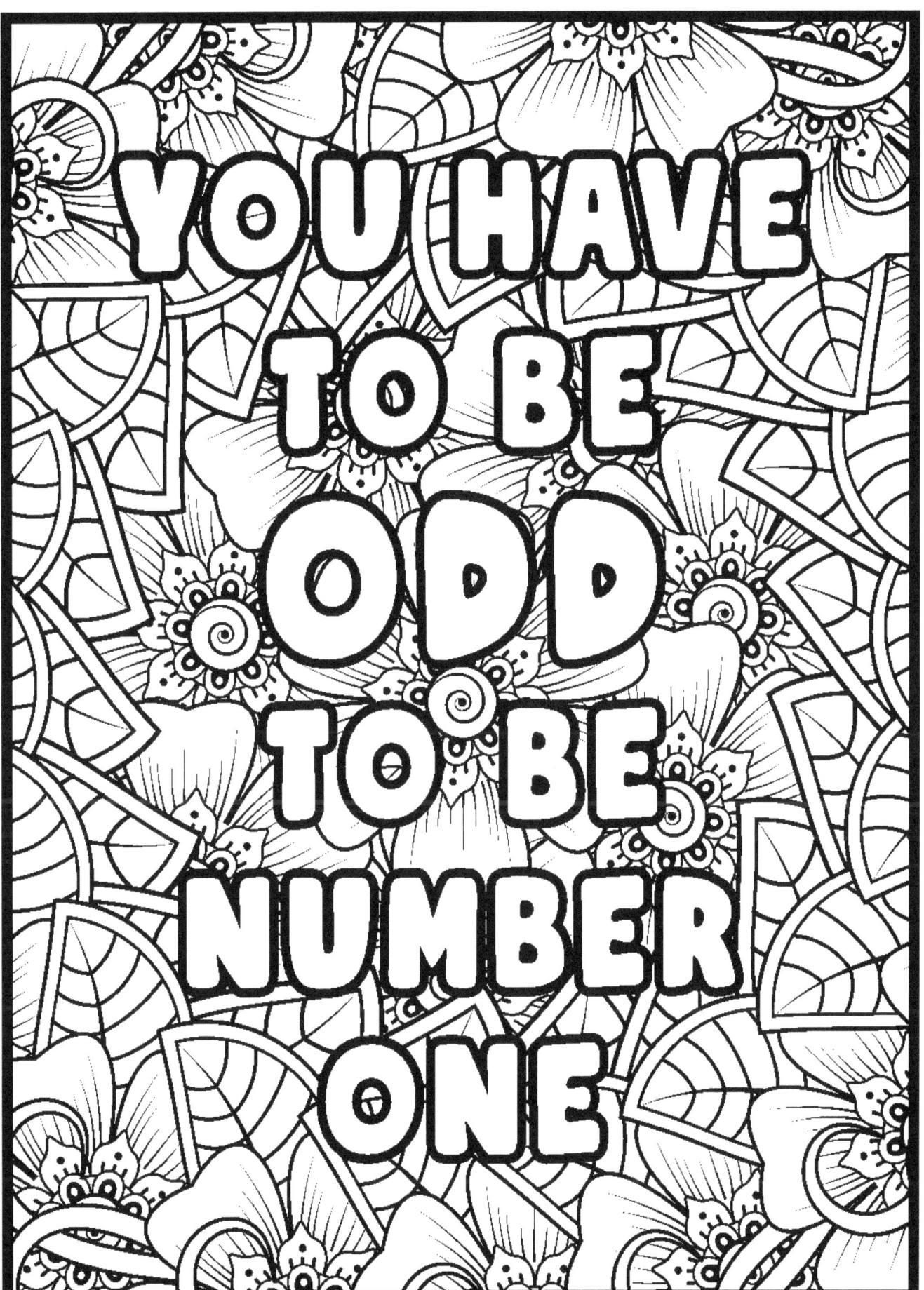

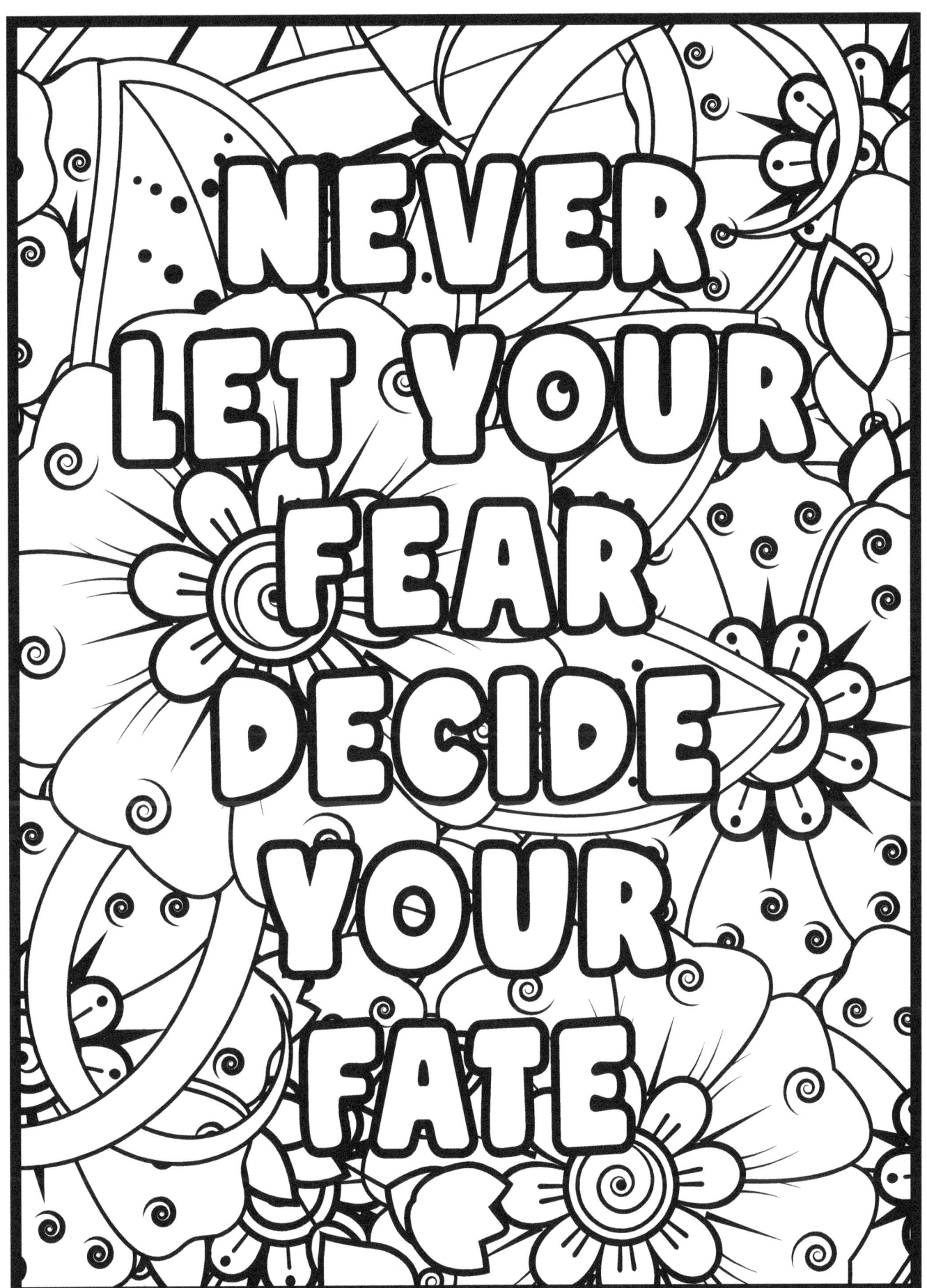

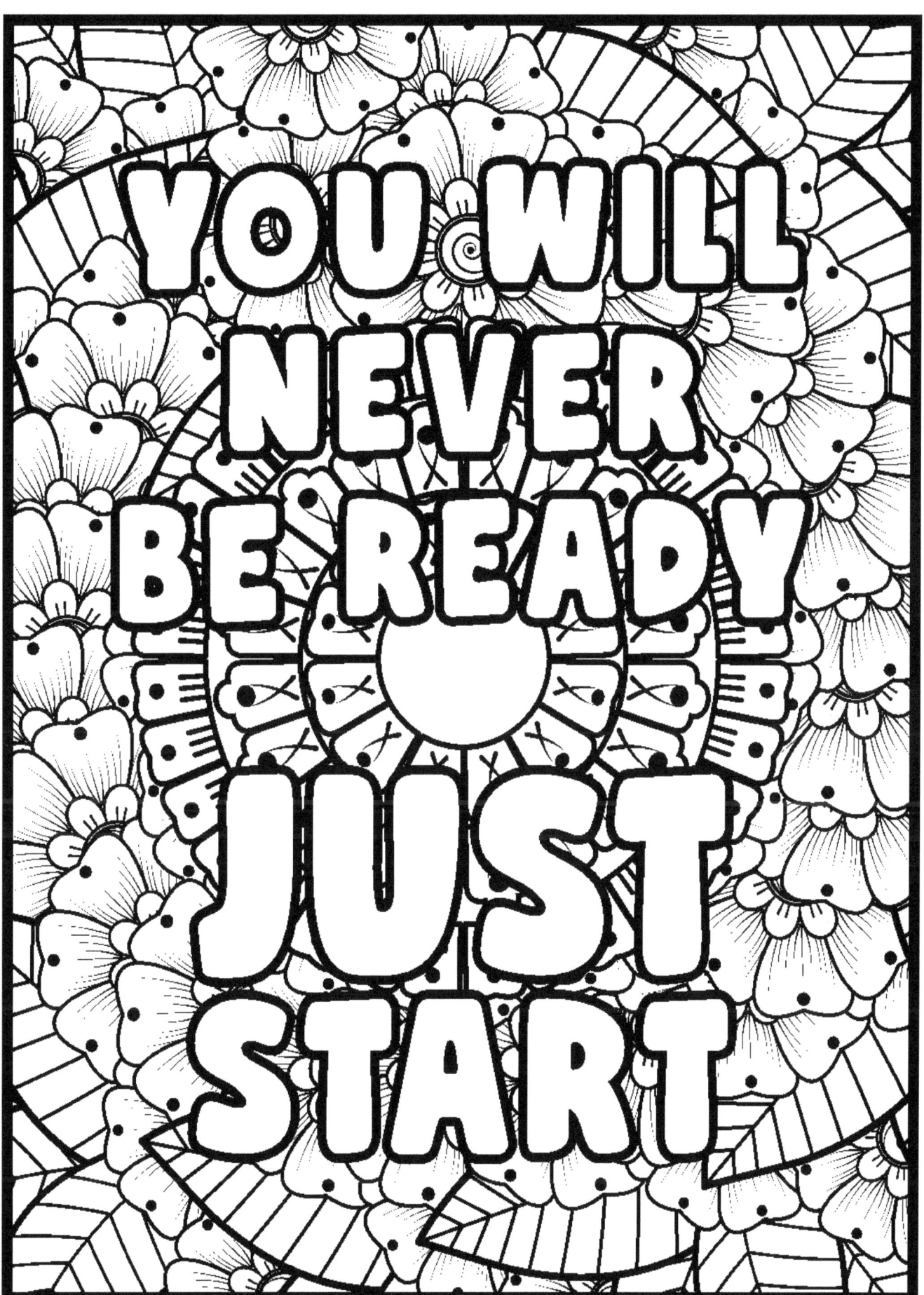

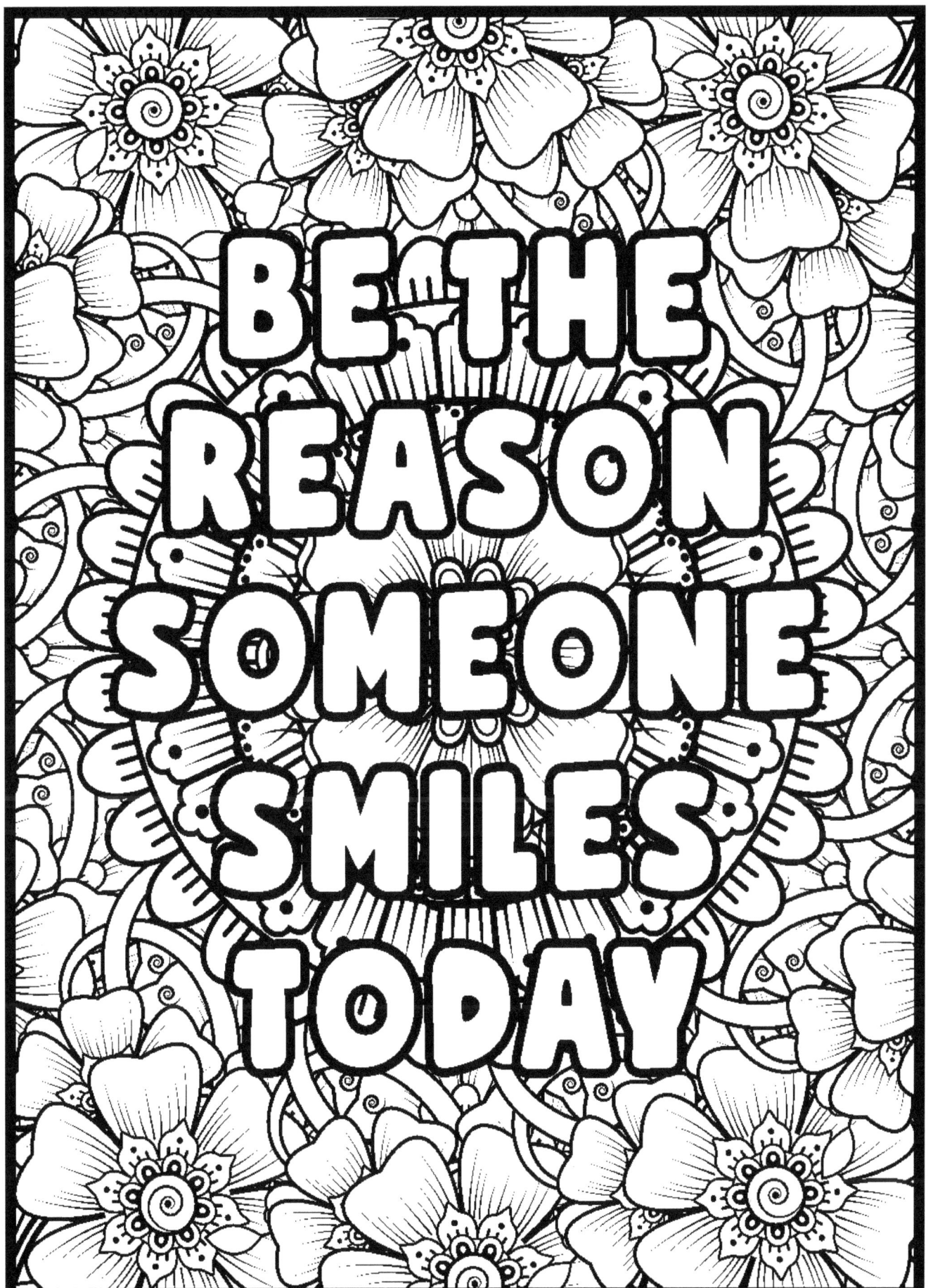

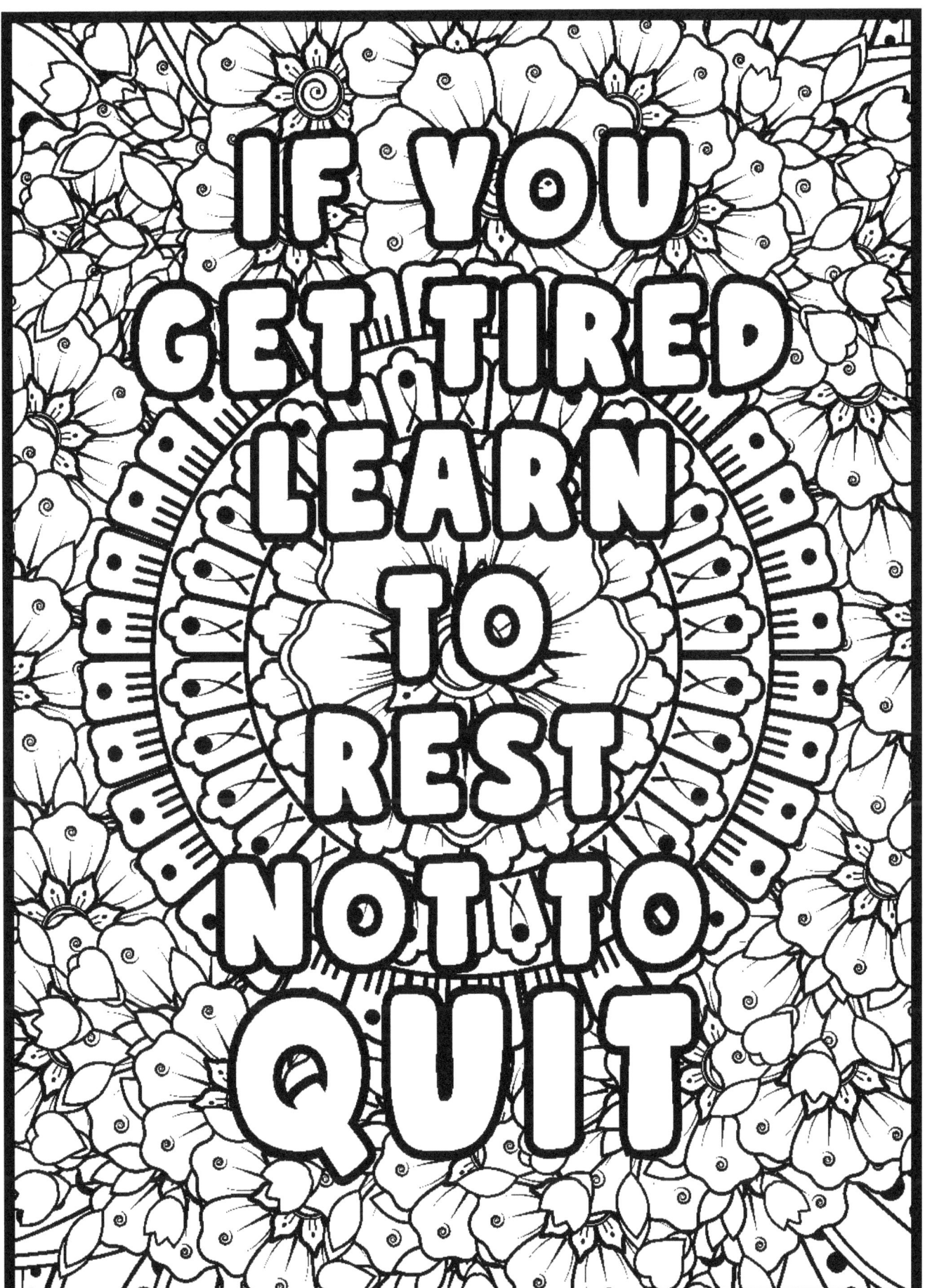

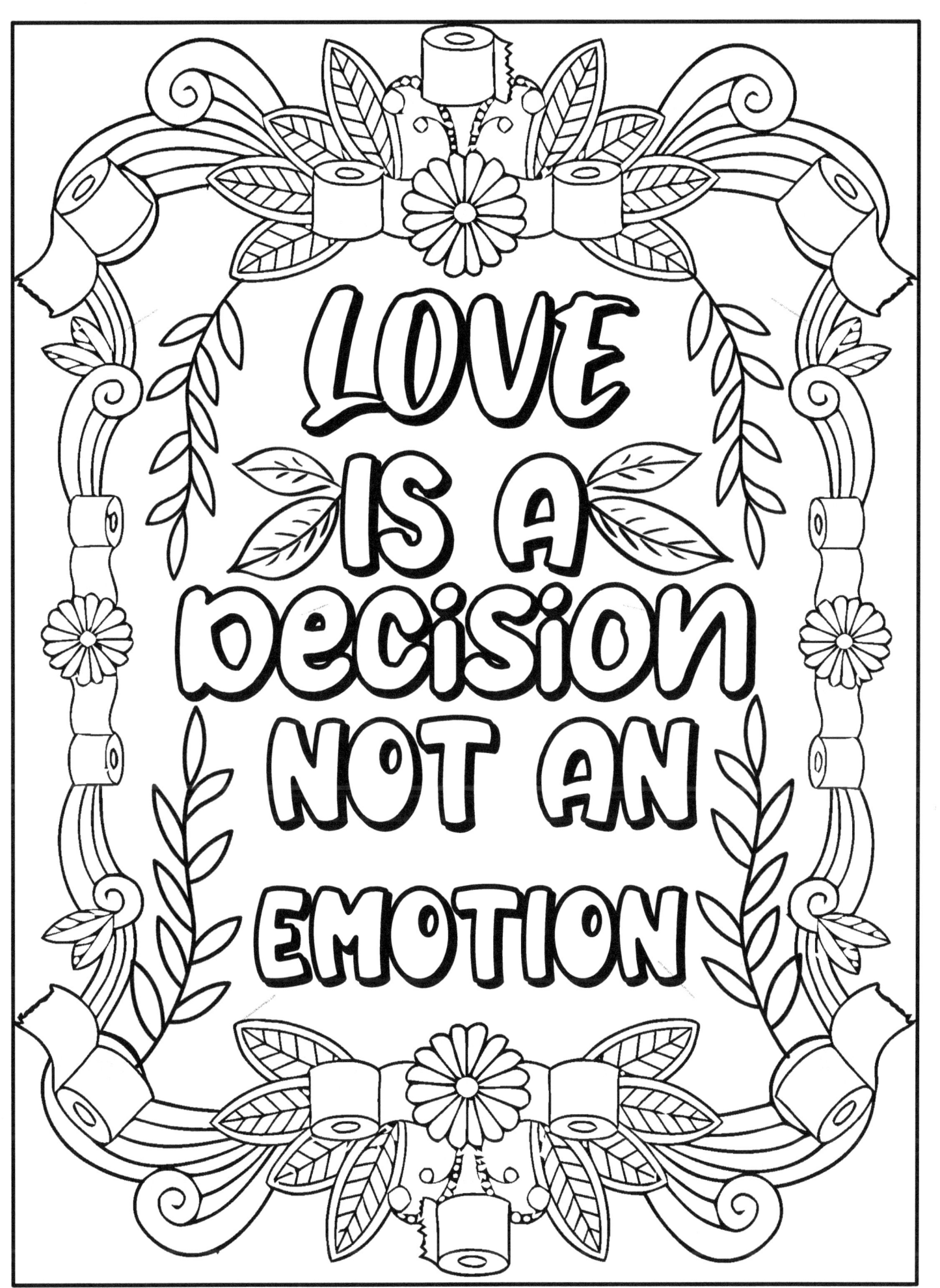

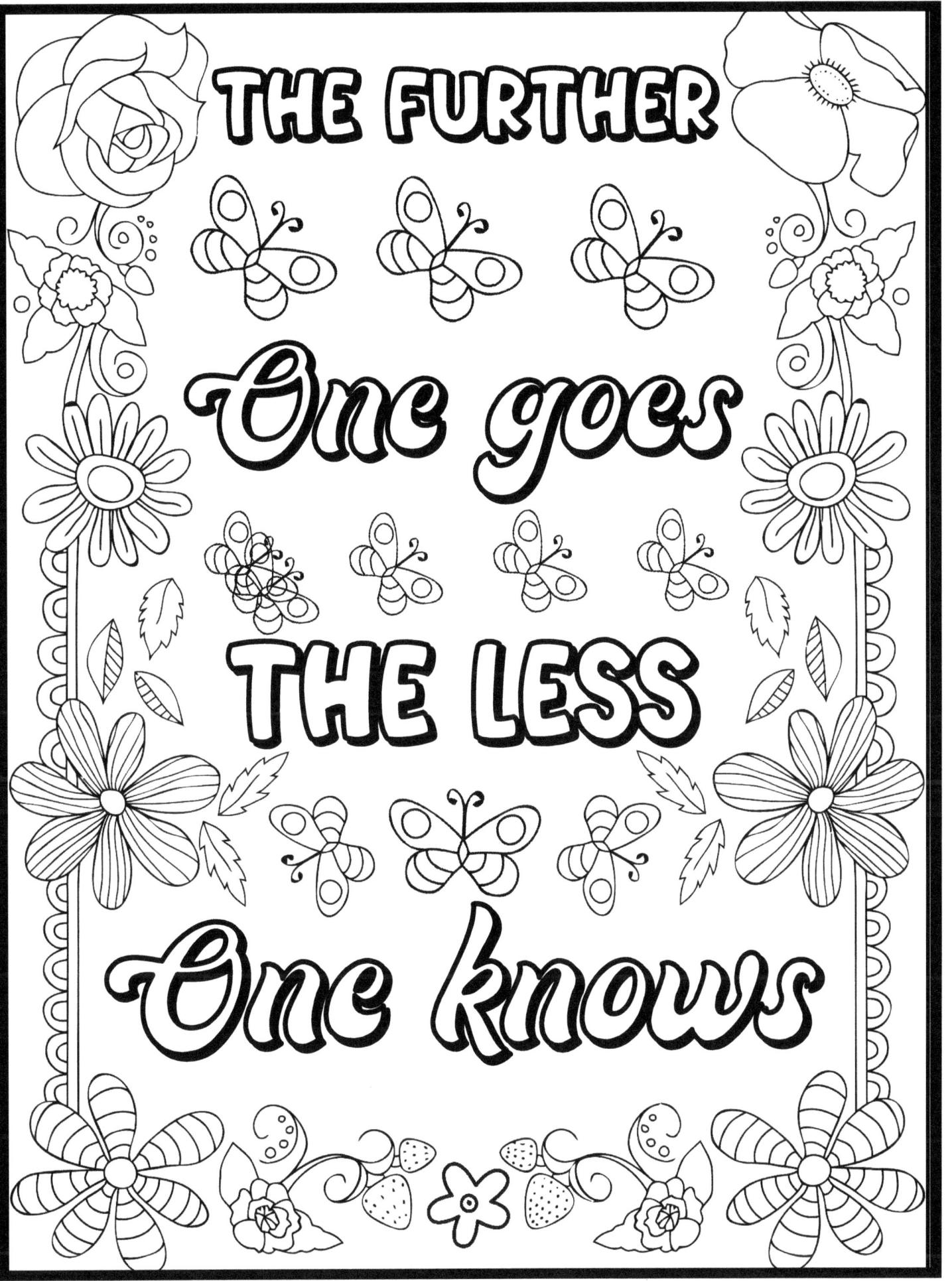

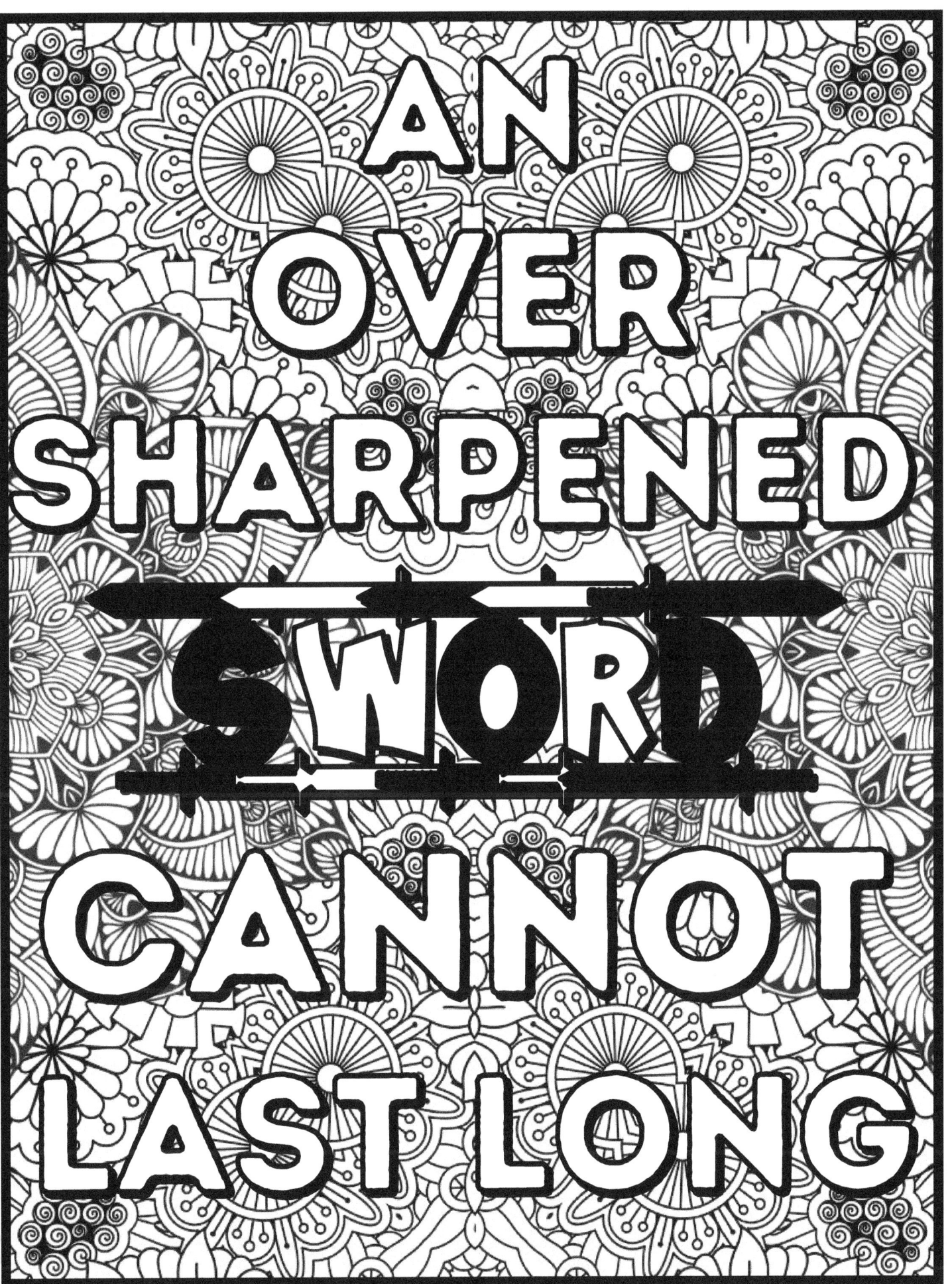

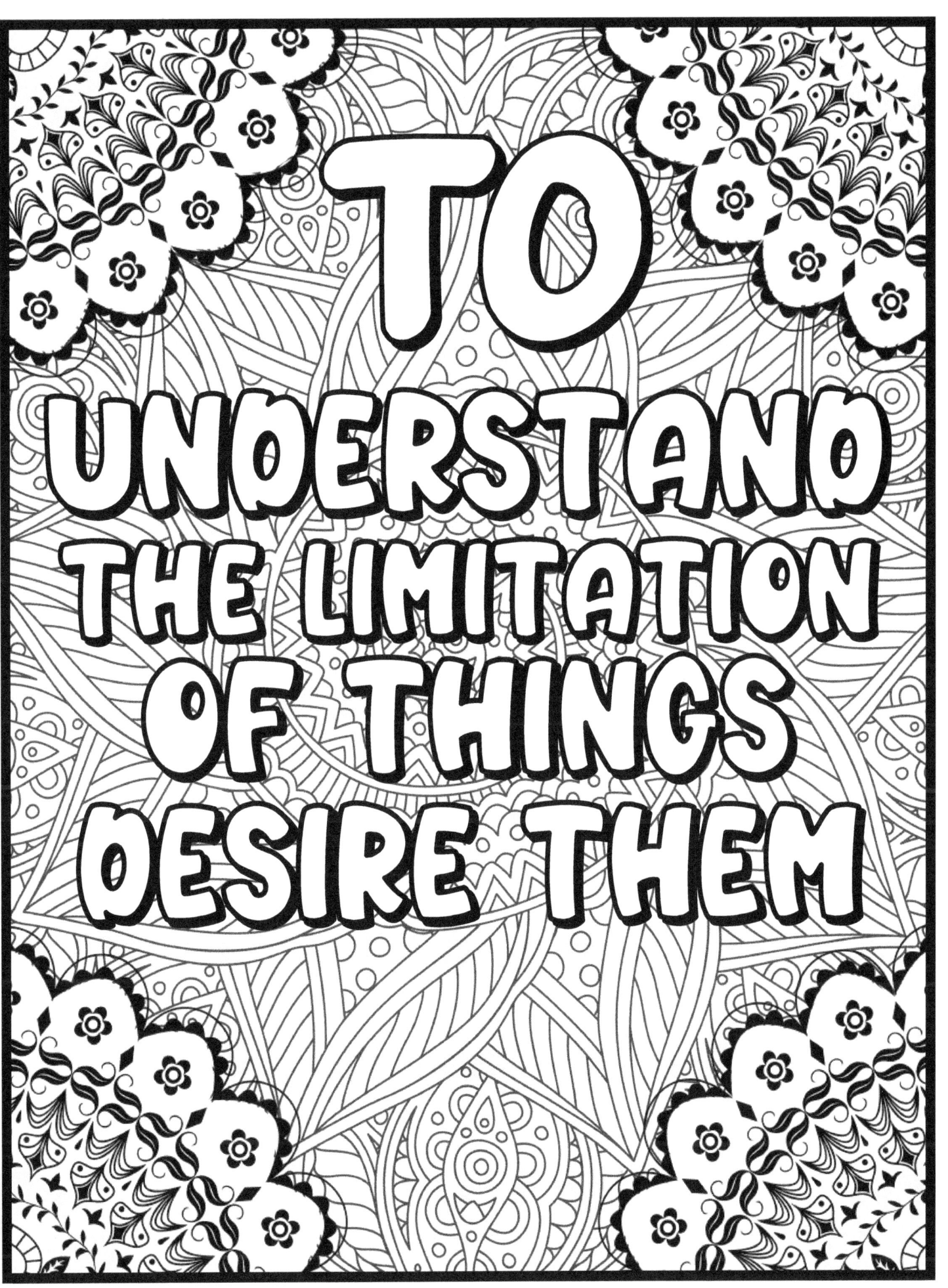

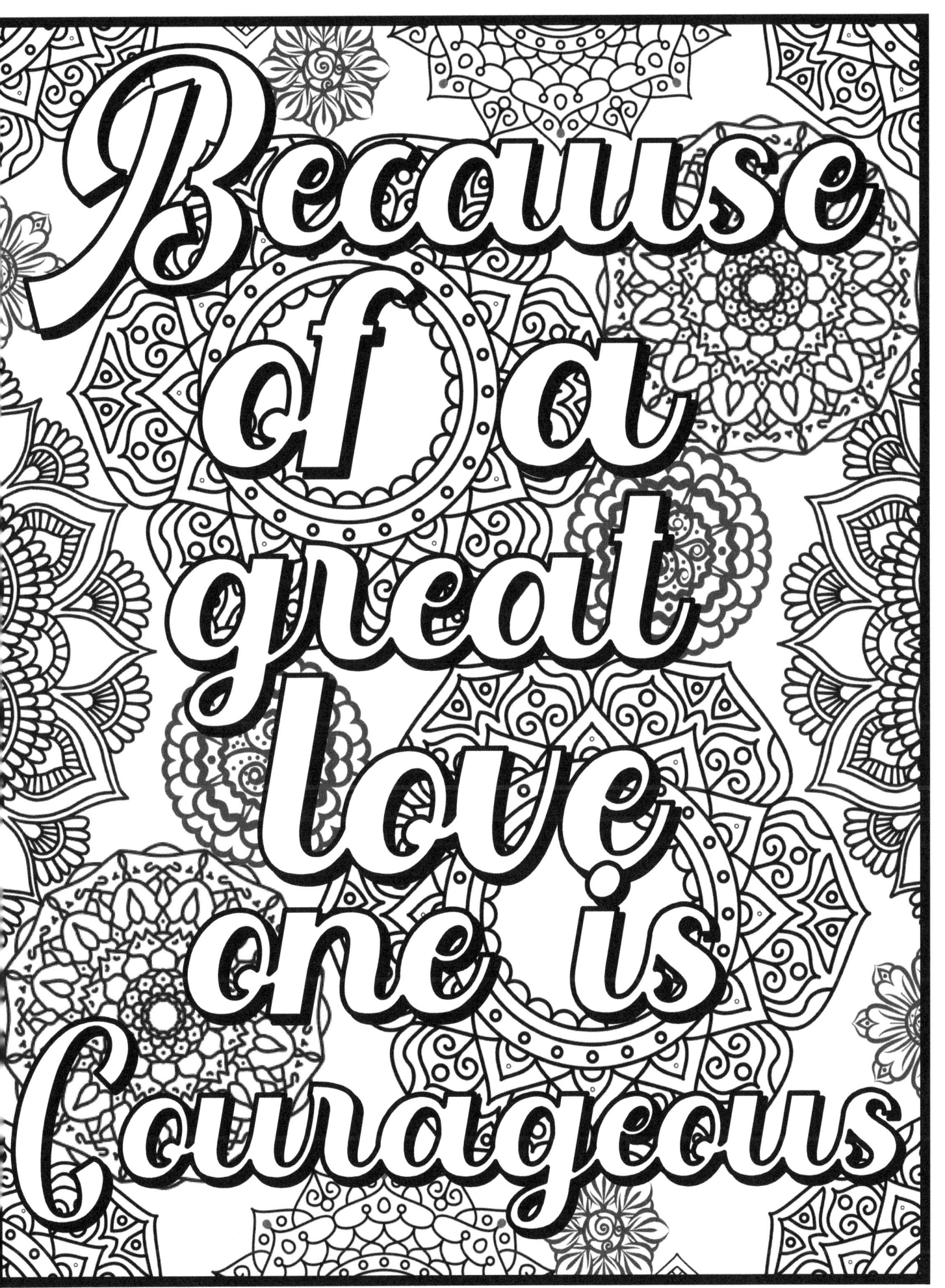

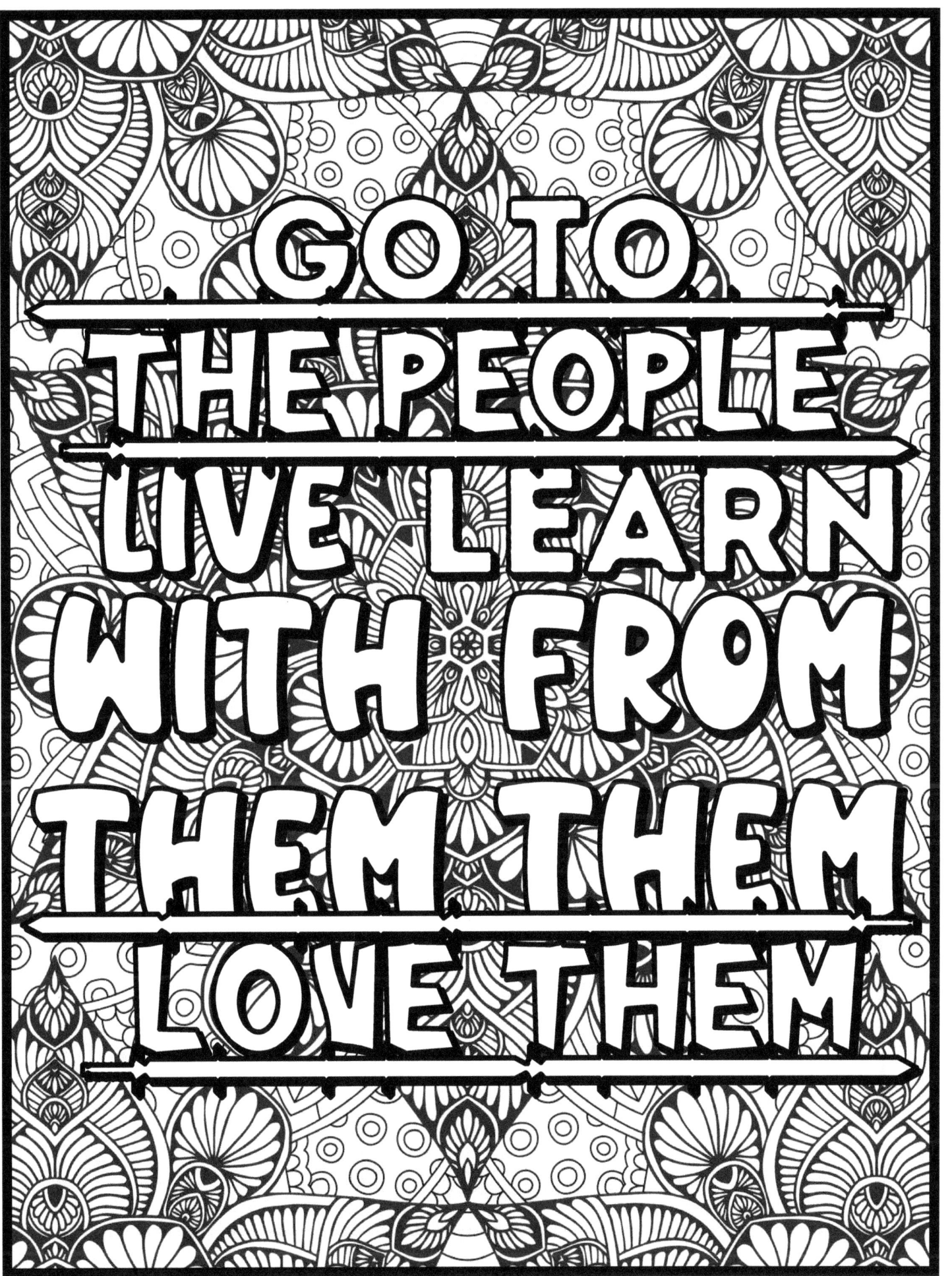

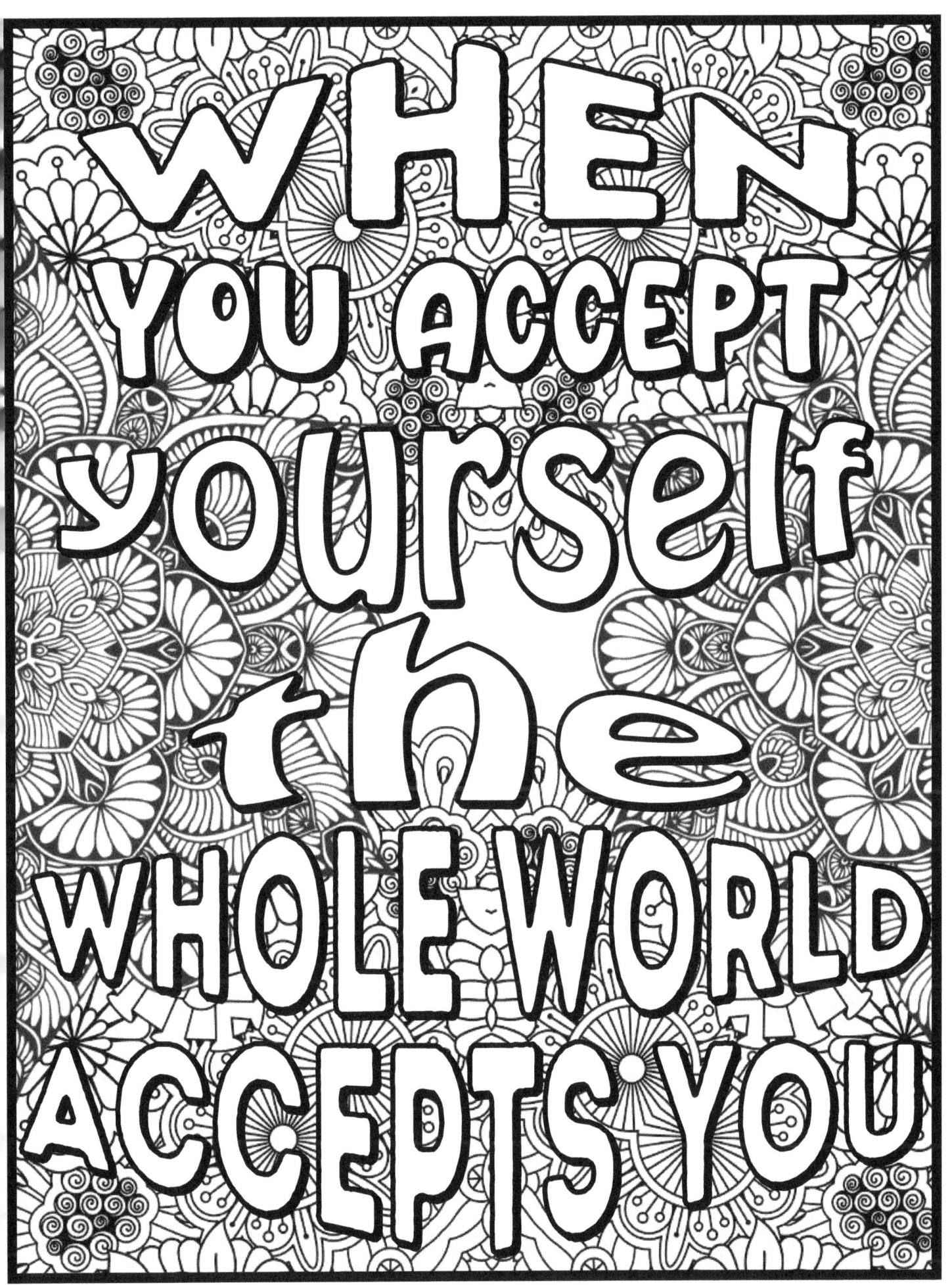

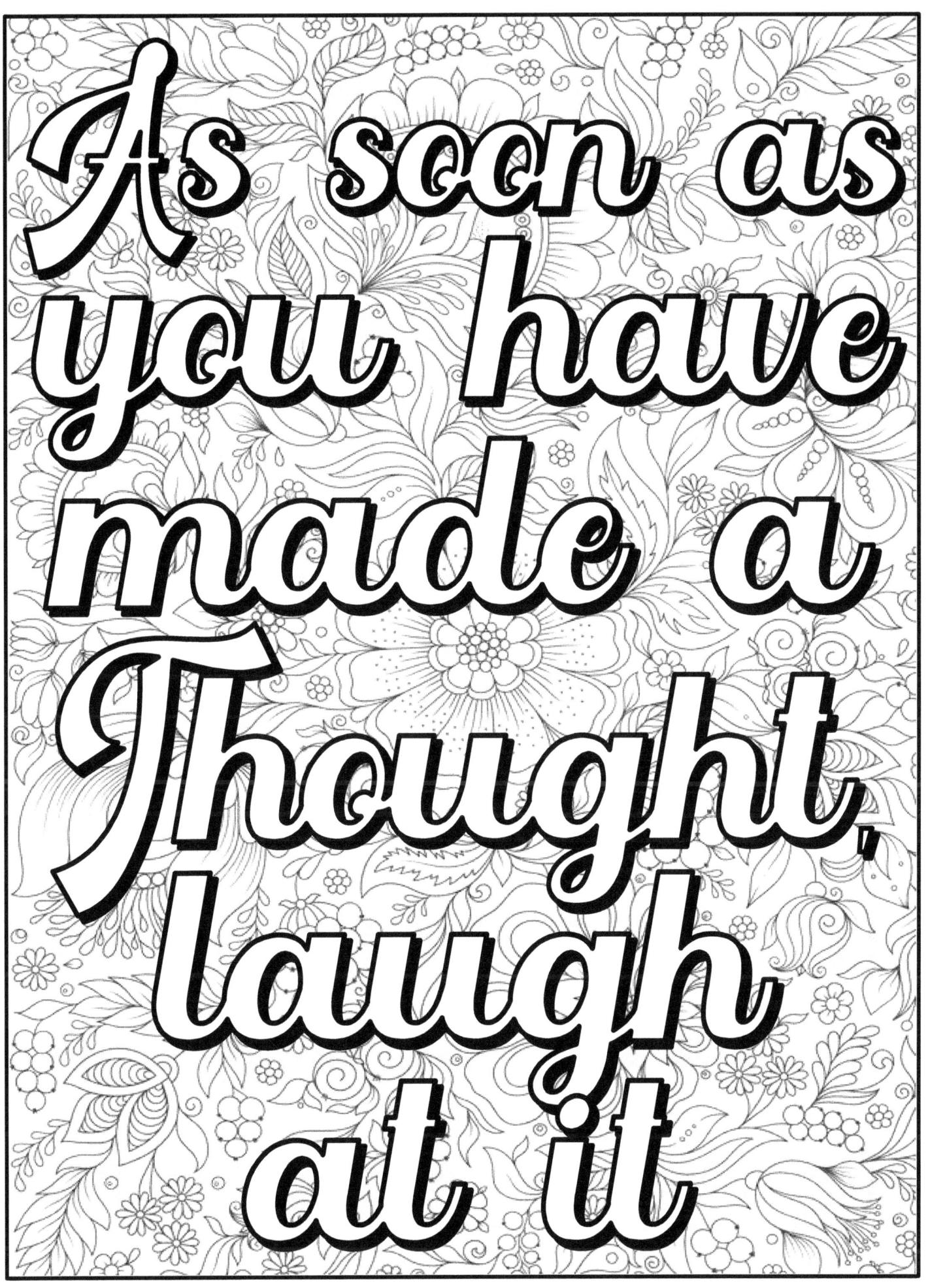

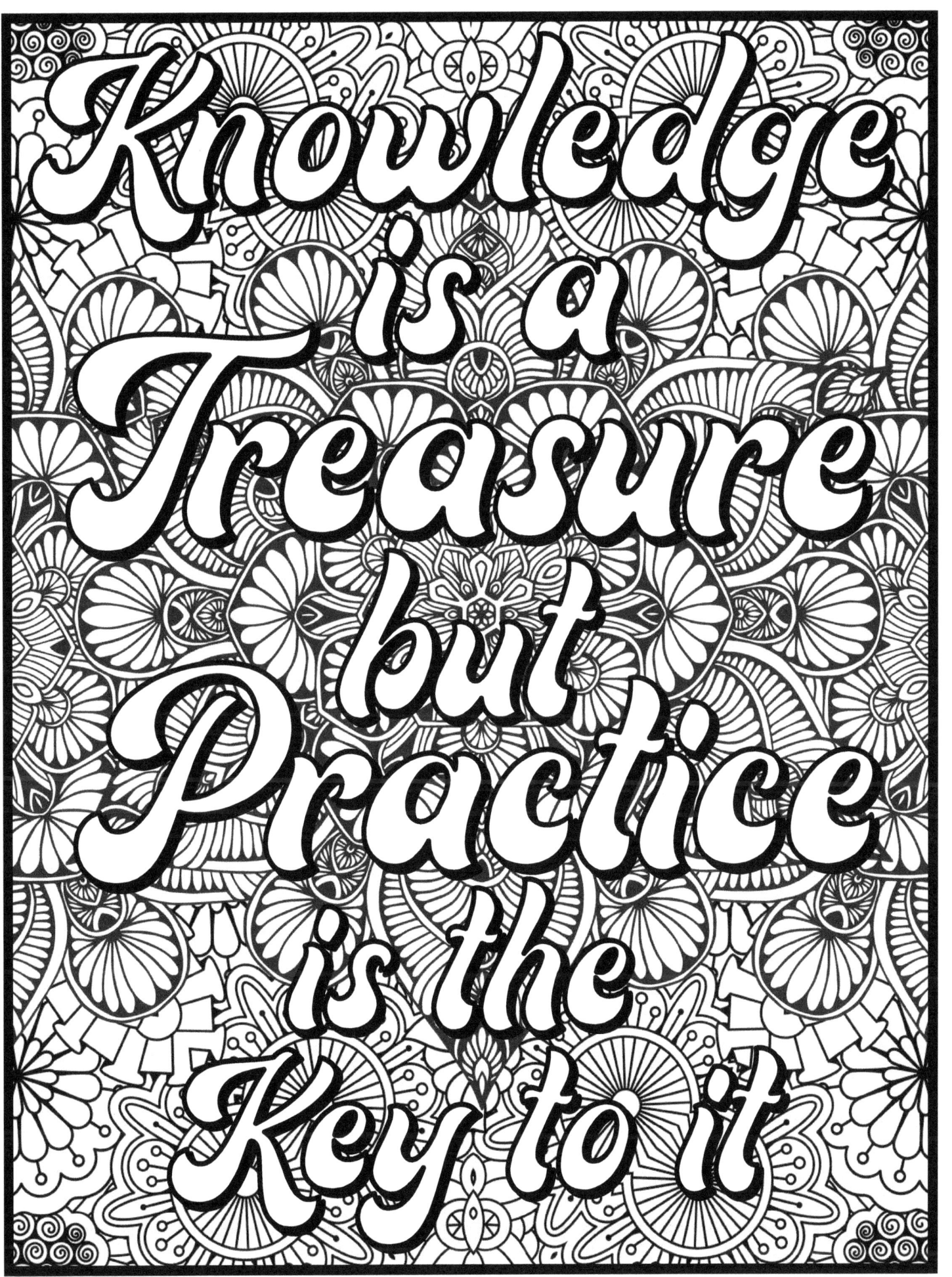

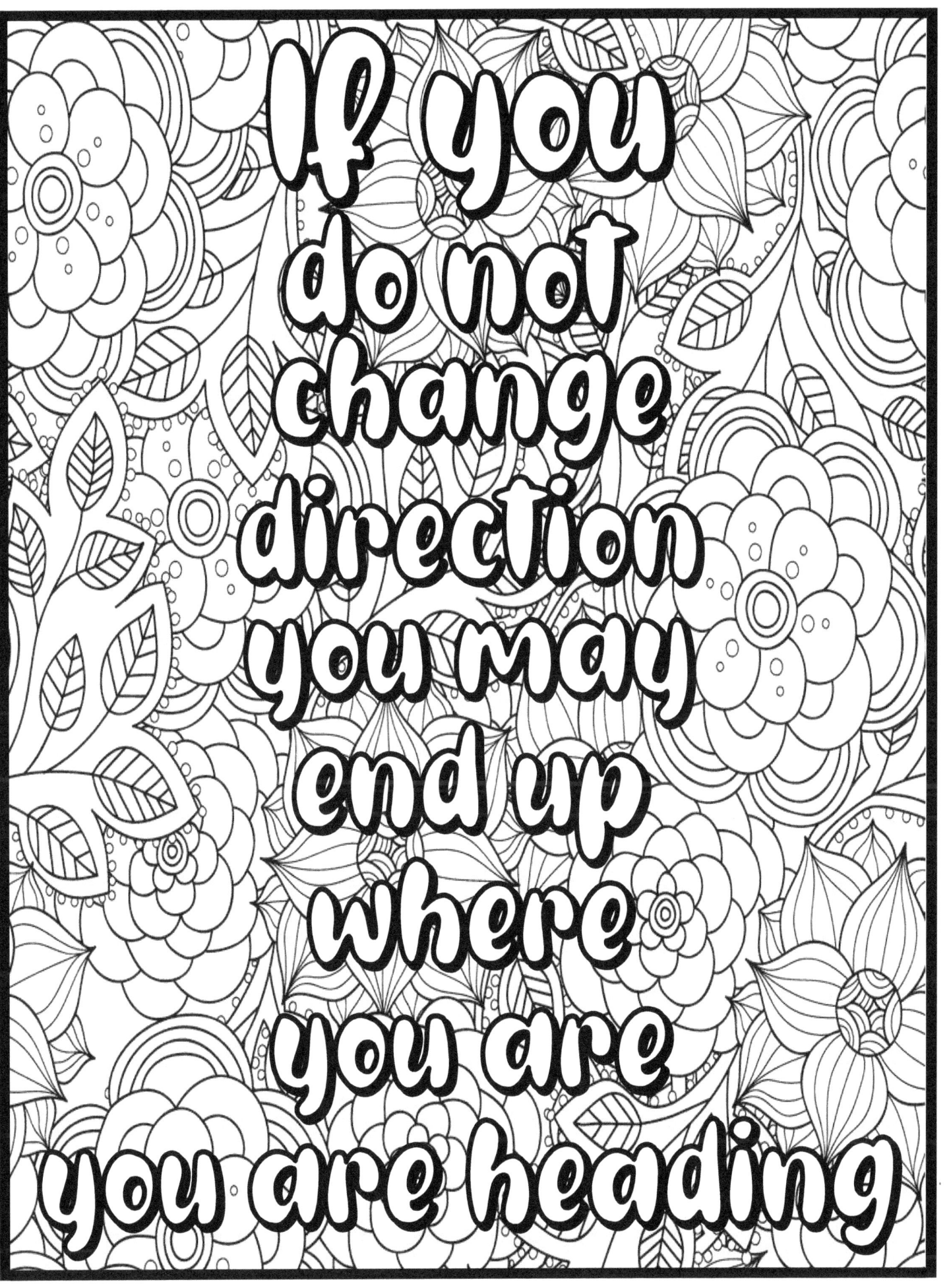

SINCERE WORDS ARE NOT FINE FINE WORDS ARE NOT SINCERE

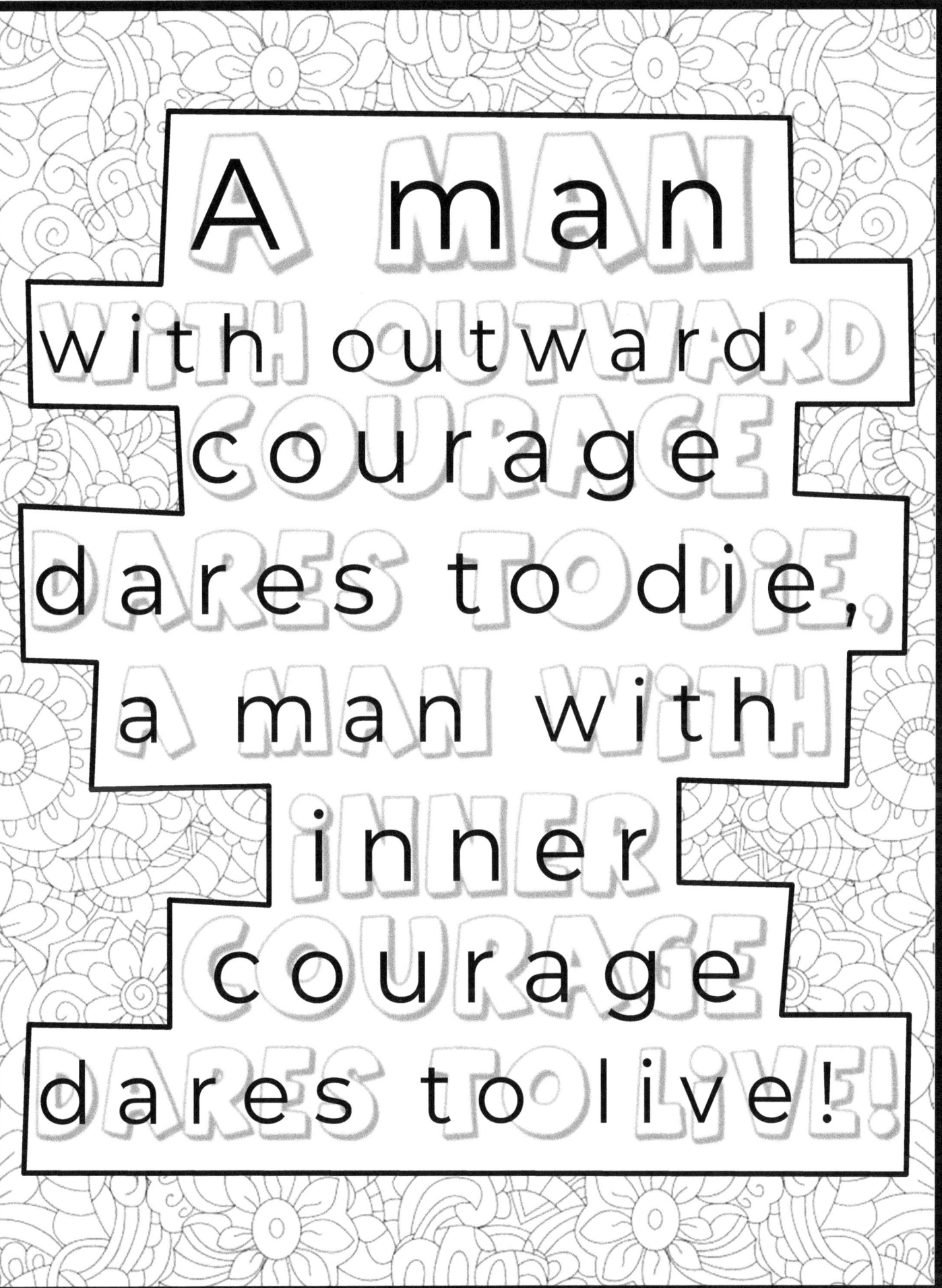

A man with outward courage dares to die, a man with inner courage dares to live!

THE SNOW GOOSE NEED NOT BATHE TO MAKE ITSELF **WHITE** NEITHER NEED YOU DO ANYTHING BUT *be yourself*

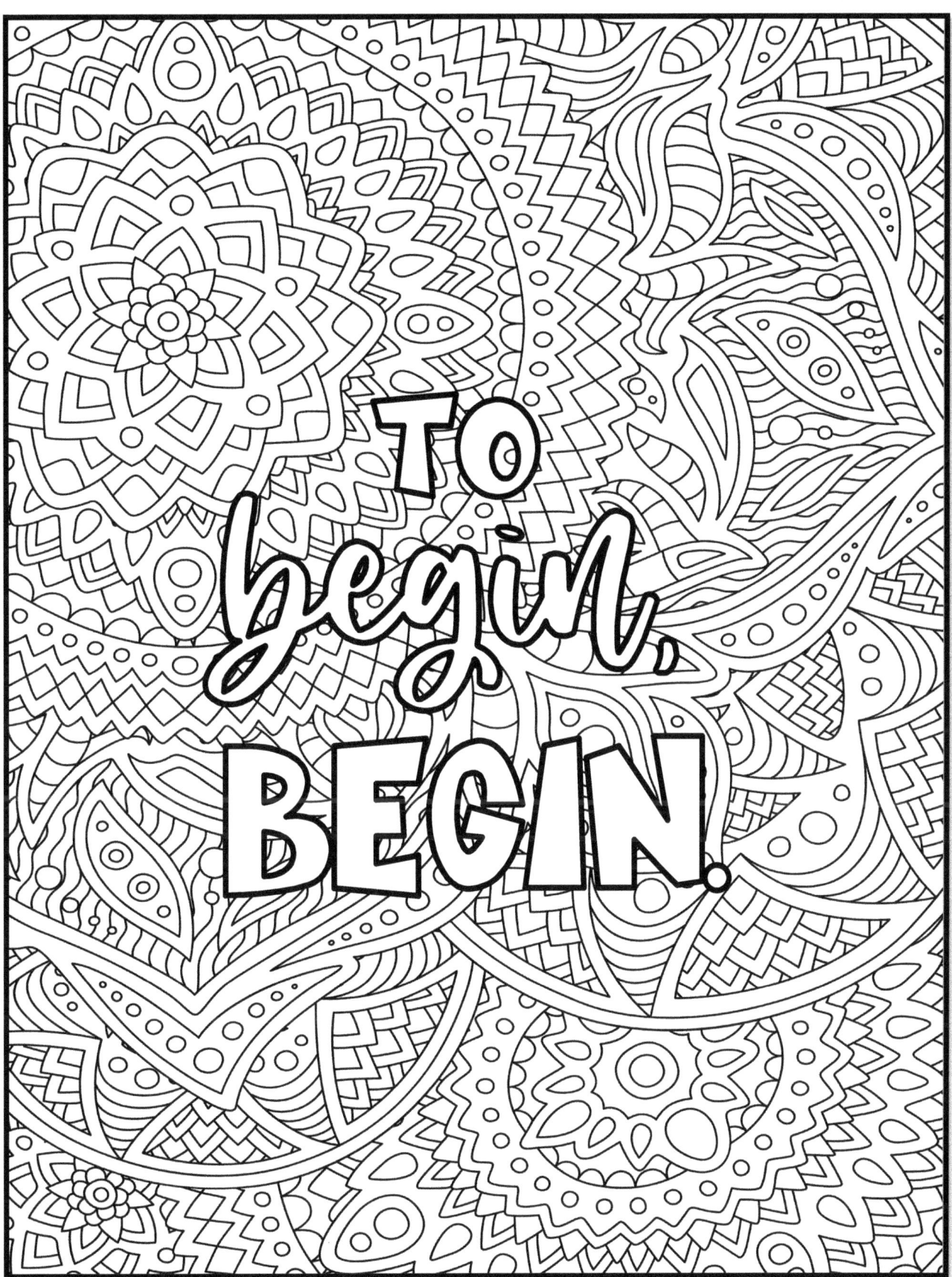

Thank You!

We create our books with love and great care.

Your opinion will help us to improve this book and create new ones.

We love to hear from you.

Please, support us and leave a review!

CPSIA information can be obtained
at www.ICGtesting.com
Printed in the USA
BVHW061043090821
613997BV00014B/444